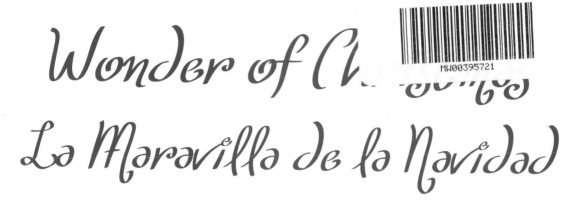

# Wonder of Christmas

# La Maravilla de la Navidad

Copyright © 2004 by Abingdon Press
All rights reserved

No part of this work may be reproduced or transmitted in any form or by any means, electronic or mechanical, including photocopying and recording, or by any information storage or retrieval system, except as may be expressly permitted by the 1976 Copyright Act or by permission in writing from the publisher. Requests for permission should be submitted in writing to: Abingdon Press, 201 Eighth Avenue South, P.O. Box 801, Nashville, Tennessee 37203, faxed to 615-749-6128, or sent via email to permission@abingdonpress.com.

Scripture quotations are from the New Revised Standard Version of the Bible. Copyright © 1989 by the Division of Christian Education of the National Council of Churches of Christ in the U.S.A. Used by permission.

Las citas bíblicas son tomadas de *La Santa Biblia, Reina-Valera, Revisión de 1995, Edición de estudio,* derechos de autor © 1995 Sociedades Bíblicas Unidas. Usado con permiso.

**ISBN 0-687-07685-4**

English text by Peg Augustine
Texto en español por Emmanuel Vargas

Illustrated by Nancy Munger
Cover and book design by Paige Easter
Cover art by Florence Davis

04 05 06 07 08 09 10 11 12 13 – 10 9 8 7 6 5 4 3 2

Manufactured in the United States of America

Abingdon Press
Nashville

*I* wonder how Mary and Joseph felt on that long trip to Bethlehem. They must have been tired, but I think they must have been excited too. They were going to visit the town of Joseph's relatives, and they were waiting for their very own baby.

*In those days a decree went out from Emperor Augustus that all the world should be registered. All went to their own towns to be registered. Joseph also went from the town of Nazareth in Galilee . . . to the city of David called Bethlehem, because he was descended from the house and family of David. He went to be registered with Mary, . . . who was expecting a child.*
Luke 2:1-5

Dear God, thank you for families who love us and care for us. Thank you for visits with grandparents and cousins. Help us to find ways to help people who do not have families. Amen.

Me imagino cómo se habrán sentido María y José después de ese largo viaje hasta Belén. Deben haber estado muy cansados, pero creo que también estaban muy emocionados. Iban a visitar el pueblo de donde era José y estaban esperando a su primer bebé.

Aconteció en aquellos días que se promulgó un edicto de parte de Augusto César, que todo el mundo fuera empadronado... E iban todos para ser empadronados, cada uno a su ciudad. También José subió de Galilea, de la ciudad de Nazaret, a Judea, a la ciudad de David, que se llama Belén, por cuanto era de la casa y familia de David, para ser empadronado con María su mujer...
la cual estaba encinta.
Lucas 2:1-5

Amado Dios, gracias por las familias que nos aman y cuidan. Gracias por las visitas de nuestros abuelos y primos. Ayúdanos a encontrar maneras de ayudar a la gente que no tiene familia. Amén.

*I* wonder what the innkeeper thought when he saw Mary and Joseph at the door. He must have been busy with all the people staying at the inn. It was very kind of him to find Mary a place to sleep in his stable.

*While they were there, the time came for her to deliver her child. And she gave birth to her firstborn son and wrapped him in bands of cloth, and laid him in a manger, because there was no place for them in the inn.*
*Luke 2:6-7*

Dear God, thank you for people who are kind to us when we have troubles. Help us to be kind to other people. Amen.

e imagino lo que debe haber pensado el mesonero cuando vio a María y José llegar hasta su puerta. Debe haber estado muy ocupado con toda la gente que estaba en su mesón. Pero fue muy amable al encontrarle un lugar a María para que pasara la noche en el establo.

*Aconteció que estando ellos allí se le cumplieron los días de su alumbramiento. Y dio a luz a su hijo primogénito, y lo envolvió en pañales y lo acostó en un pesebre, porque no había lugar para ellos en el mesón.*
*Lucas 2:6-7*

Amado Dios, gracias por las personas que nos ayudan cuando tenemos problemas. Permítenos ayudar a las personas que lo necesiten. Amén.

*I* wonder if there were other people sleeping in the stable that night. There might have been, or maybe there were only the animals who always slept there. They must have made it cozy and warm.

*Every generous act of giving, with every perfect gift, is from above.*
*James 1:17*

Dear God, thank you for beds and cozy places to sleep. Help us to remember those people who don't have homes. Show us ways to help them. Amen.

$\mathcal{M}$e imagino si habría otras personas durmiendo en el establo esa noche. Probablemente sí, o tal vez solamente estaban los animales que siempre dormían ahí. Esos animales hacían que el establo fuera confortable y calientito.

Toda buena dádiva y todo don
perfecto desciende de lo alto.
Santiago 1:17

Amado Dios, gracias por las camas y lugares agradables para dormir. Ayúdanos a recordar a quienes no tienen casa. Y muéstranos maneras de poder ayudarlos. Amén.

*I* wonder how many angels sang in the sky that night. There must have been a lot. The Bible says it was a multitude. Their song must have sounded even more beautiful than the ones our choir sings at Christmas. I wish I could hear angels sing!

In that region there were shepherds living in the fields, keeping watch over their flock by night. Then an angel of the Lord stood before them, and the glory of the Lord shone around them, and they were terrified. But the angel said to them, "Do not be afraid; for see—I am bringing you good news of great joy . . . to you is born . . . a Savior, . . . you will find a child wrapped in bands of cloth and lying in a manger." And suddenly there was with the angel a multitude of the heavenly host, praising God and saying, "Glory to God in the highest heaven, and on earth peace . . . ."
Luke 2:8-14

Dear God, thank you for music! Help us to remember to say thank you to the people who sing in worship. Help us to work for peace in your world. Amen.

Me imagino cuántos ángeles habrán cantado en el cielo esa noche. ¡Deben haber sido muchos! La Biblia dice que era una multitud. Sus cantos deben haberse escuchado mucho más hermosos que los que el coro de la iglesia canta en Navidad. ¡Cómo me gustaría oír cantar a los ángeles!

Había pastores en la misma región, que velaban y guardaban las vigilias de la noche sobre su rebaño. Y se les presentó un ángel del Señor y la gloria del Señor los rodeó de resplandor, y tuvieron gran temor. Pero el ángel les dijo:
—No temáis, porque yo os doy nuevas de gran gozo, que será para todo el pueblo: que os ha nacido hoy... un Salvador... Hallaréis al niño envuelto en pañales, acostado en un pesebre. Repentinamente apareció con el ángel una multitud de las huestes celestiales, que alababan a Dios y decían:
«¡Gloria a Dios en las alturas y en la tierra paz...!».
Lucas 2:8-14

Amado Dios, ¡gracias por la música! Ayúdanos a recordar dar las gracias a las personas que cantan en el culto. Ayúdanos a trabajar para que haya paz en tu mundo. Amén.

*I* wonder if all the shepherds went to Bethlehem to see the baby. Maybe one stayed behind with the sheep. They must have been excited about the good news the angels brought. The Bible says they hurried to Bethlehem.

When the angels had left them and gone into heaven, the shepherds said to one another, "Let us go now to Bethlehem and see this thing that has taken place, which the Lord has made known to us." So they went with haste and found Mary and Joseph, and the child lying in the manger.
Luke 2:15-16

Dear God, thank you for your gift of Jesus. We are proud to be his followers and to be called Christians. Amen.

Me imagino si todos los pastores habrán ido a Belén a ver al bebé. Tal vez uno se quedó para vigilar a las ovejas. Deben haber estado muy emocionados con las buenas noticias que el ángel les anunció. La Biblia dice que se apresuraron para ir a Belén.

Sucedió que cuando los ángeles se fueron de ellos al cielo, los pastores se dijeron unos a otros:
—Pasemos, pues, hasta Belén, y veamos esto que ha sucedido y que el Señor nos ha manifestado.
Vinieron, pues, apresuradamente, y hallaron a María y a José, y al niño acostado en el pesebre.
Lucas 2:15-16

Amado Dios, gracias por tu regalo que es Jesús. Estamos orgullosos de ser sus seguidores y de ser llamados cristianos. Amén.

*I* wonder what the people thought when they heard the shepherds going back to their sheep. The shepherds told everyone about the good news the baby in the manger was bringing to all people. The people in Bethlehem must have been as excited as the shepherds.

They made known what had been told them about this child; and all who heard it were amazed at what the shepherds told them. The shepherds returned, glorifying and praising God for all they had heard and seen, as it had been told them.
Luke 2:17-18, 20

Dear God, thank you for the shepherds who told other people about Jesus. Help us to share the good news with all people everywhere. Amen.

Me imagino qué pensó la gente cuando vieron a los pastores regresar a donde estaban sus ovejas. Los pastores les dijeron a todos sobre las buenas noticias que el bebé del pesebre estaba trayendo para todo el mundo. La gente en Belén debe haber estado igual de emocionada que los pastores.

*Al verlo, dieron a conocer lo que se les había dicho acerca del niño. Todos los que oyeron, se maravillaron de lo que los pastores les decían... Los pastores se volvieron glorificando y alabando a Dios por todas las cosas que habían oído y visto, como se les había dicho.*
*Lucas 2:17-18, 20*

Amado Dios, gracias por los pastores que les contaron a las otras personas sobre Jesús. Ayúdanos a compartir las buenas nuevas con toda la gente en todos los lugares. Amén.

*I* wonder how far the wise men had to travel. It must have been a long, long way. The star must have shone very brightly to lead them on their way.

After Jesus was born in Bethlehem . . . wise men from the East came to Jerusalem, asking, "Where is the child who has been born king of the Jews? For we observed his star at its rising, and have come to pay him homage." When they saw that the star had stopped, they were overwhelmed with joy. On entering the house, they saw the child . . . and they knelt down and paid him homage. Then, opening their treasure chests, they offered him gifts of gold, frankincense, and myrrh.
Matthew 2:1-2, 10-11

Dear God, thank you for the wise men who traveled a long way to worship Jesus. Thank you for the gifts we receive at Christmas. Show us how to give to others. Help us to remember every day to praise you and to remember Jesus' love for us. Amen.

Me imagino qué tan lejos tuvieron que viajar los sabios del Oriente. Debe haber sido un largo, largo camino. La estrella debe haber brillado mucho para poder dirigirlos en su sendero.

Cuando Jesús nació, en Belén..., llegaron del oriente a Jerusalén unos sabios, preguntando:
—¿Dónde está el rey de los judíos que ha nacido?, pues su estrella hemos visto en el oriente y venimos a adorarlo...
Y al ver la estrella, se regocijaron con muy grande gozo. Al entrar en la casa, vieron al niño ...y postrándose lo adoraron. Luego, abriendo sus tesoros, le ofrecieron presentes: oro, incienso y mirra.
Mateo 2:1-2, 10-11

Amado Dios, gracias por los sabios del Oriente que viajaron tanto solamente para adorar a Jesús. Gracias por los regalos que recibimos en Navidad. Pero también enséñanos a dar regalos a otras personas. Ayúdanos a que todos los días te adoremos y a recordar el amor de Jesús por nosotros. Amén.

*I* wonder if the wise men kept watching the stars when they got back home. They must have known they would never see such a star again. But their journey had ended just as they wanted it to—they met the new King of all the earth.

And having been warned in a dream not
to return to Herod,
they left for their own country by another road.
Matthew 2:12

Dear God, thank you for the world you created— for the sun, and the moon, and the stars. Help us to be like stars, pointing the way to Jesus. Amen.